The GHETTO is a LIE

LEARN HOW TO GET GRITTY AND
STAY GRITTY WHEN THE CARDS ARE
STACKED AGAINST YOU

by Cozette Church Gaston, PhD

Dedication

I dedicate this book to my husband, Damien Maurice Gaston, and my two children, Damien Tyan Gaston and Londyn Simone Nakia Gaston. Although you have witnessed my lowest moments in life, you never left my side and you never devalued me. I firmly believe that God allowed me to experience a cohesive family with you because the three of you taught me how to love unconditionally and how to be vulnerable even when it hurts to experience actual growth. I love you!

I also dedicate this book to John "Papa Art" Freeman. Although you are no longer with us, your spirit continues to live in us! I will never forget the words you spoke to me right before I experienced a prophylactic bilateral mastectomy. You said, "You will be alright little momma." It was at that moment I knew that you would always watch over me. You will never leave my heart!

Acknowledgments

I would like to extend my appreciation to Dr. Marla Sheppard, Deputy Superintendent of Kansas City Public Schools. You have helped me in so many ways. I will never forget how you encouraged me to look deeply into my soul in an effort to define my authenticity. You also encouraged me to courageously reflect on any past mistakes to learn from them so that I could experience a better day, week, month, and year. Yes, I genuinely believe that you teach what you model, and I surely learned a lot about leadership from you based on what you modeled in the District!

I would also like to thank my parents for supporting my passion to travel a different path. Both of you never got in my way when I expressed a desire to go out and get something that appeared to be far-fetched. Thank you for believing in me and my vision to be the best version of myself.

I would like to thank my line sisters from the Delta Pi Chapter of Delta Sigma Theta Sorority, Incorporated. You ladies have been my biggest supporters over the last few years. I am appreciative of our sisterhood, our bond, and our friendship. *Oh to be a Delta girl!*

Lastly, I would like to thank my closest friends, who I often call my sisters. You know who you are because of all the special moments we have shared. Thank you for your transparency, heart, and *girl talk* time!

Table Of Contents

Dedication iii

Acknowledgments v

Introduction.. ix

Chapter One: Don't Settle For Hand Me Downs 1

Chapter Two: The G.h.e.t.t.o. Cover Story 8

Chapter Three: Keep It 100% 14

Chapter Four: Got Goals? 18

Chapter Five: Make Neighborhood Moves 23

Chapter Six: The Block Is Hot, Stay Woke! 27

Chapter Seven: Breathe! It Is In You To Succeed!.....................33

Chapter Eight: Develop A Deep Down Passion To Persevere.........39

Chapter Nine: Maintain An Alpha And Omega Mindset 43

Chapter Ten: Get Comfortable With Being Uncomfortable 48

Chapter Eleven: Don't Be Scared To Be The Anomaly 53

Chapter Twelve: That's Game! 56

Conclusion..60

References...61

Introduction

The *Ghetto is a Lie* highlights the struggles I have encountered from childhood into adulthood. It unveils why I was made with such a tough exterior that has shielded me during my lifespan. As a woman with a strong mindset, I have had to identify the events that have had an impact on my life, which affected my thinking process, behavior, and inability to develop healthy relationships with people.

When I looked deeply into my past, I noticed that my family issues were actually family "curses" because of the misfortune that has traveled from generation to generation surrounding diseases, domestic violence, and education. It did not begin when my parents united to form a family. It started before they were born and possibly before their parents being born. Of course, learning about these generational curses forced me to do things differently in an effort to reap a different outcome and to say, "It ends here!"

Understanding my childhood experiences forced me to look deeply into equitable practices that may have kept some family members from pursuing their dreams. I firmly believe that people who are raised in disadvantaged households receive unfair treatment and responses when attempting to acquire a high level of education and during their pursuit of upper level management positions. I also believe that in order to achieve greatness, you have to block out negative presuppositions. You have to block out past failure and you must challenge yourself to become more than naysayers thought you could become in life!

The Ghetto is a Lie will highlight twelve strategies you can employ to push past obstacles that have confronted you. *The Ghetto is a Lie* will also encourage you to reflect on your past failures in an effort to discover the learning within you to embrace your next best step.

Therefore, if you are ready for the race of your life, I dare you to approach the starting line while envisioning your ability to become unstoppable despite the cards that are stacked against you!

CHAPTER ONE

Don't Settle for Hand Me Downs

"I tell you, you can pray for anything, and if you believe that you've received it, it will be yours."

(New Living Translation, Mark. 11.24)

A s a little girl, I would often stay at home with my dad because my mom worked a first shift job. Working a first shift job positioned my dad as the caregiver during the daytime. Thus, being at home with him during the day shaped me into a daddy's girl! I looked up to my dad and considered him a hero. He was a hard worker who worked a second shift job and sometimes weekends, outgoing, and energetic. He was my daddy! He was perfect in my eyes! But, there came a time, as the years progressed, I realized that my dad was not so perfect after all. Although he worked two jobs to help make ends meet, he began to behave in a manner that was a little different for me. My dad began to assert himself in such a way that instilled fear in my heart. Of course, as a child,

I would hear people say, "Children should fear their parents." However, this fear was the type of fear that would make my bones tremble. This was the type of fear that would cause me to think about my existence. I always wondered if I would live long enough to tell my story.

As time continued to pass, I learned that the behavior I observed with my dad was due to his consumption of alcohol. Of course, my dad's consumption of alcohol appeared to be a harmless habit. However, the drinking became frequent and the frequency of alcohol consumption turned into a lifestyle. Now, this is a lot for a child to take in at such a young age. But, I had no choice. I thought it was normal. I thought it was supposed to be that way! In my worldview, seeing my dad's eyes bloodshot red, witnessing his drunken aggression, and experiencing fear were all regular occurrences in our household. Why couldn't he see how his heavy consumption of alcohol affected the family? Why couldn't we be like the neighbors across the street? These were the questions I asked myself.

It took me several years to realize that our family was an example of a dysfunctional system. It took me even longer to admit that the background of my family negatively affected my lens on life. As a child, to think of normalcy meant to consider alcoholism as a way of life. To think of normalcy meant to consider domestic violence as a way of life. To think of normalcy meant to embrace verbal abuse as a way of life. The actions described above were *my* normal. Later in life, I learned that *my* normal was not normal after all. Therefore, I had to develop a new normal. *My* new normal meant that I had to think differently. *My* new normal meant I had to behave differently. You see, when you are accustomed to maladaptive behaviors, addictions, and unfavorable circumstances, you have to be very intentional about changing who you are as a person. That means, you must be aware of what needs to be changed to experience the new you! It was no longer good enough for me to live in the same household with my father because I was forced to embrace his persistent absenteeism at my track meets due to the alcohol addiction. What I considered as normal was indeed abnormal and I declared to be different than the normal I knew.

In this book, you will learn about how my mother experienced domestic abuse and how her experience with abuse caused her to unknowingly project abusive behaviors towards other people. Although I have witnessed alcohol abuse and domestic violence, I knew I needed to develop a new mindset to become the person God desired me to become. Having a microscopic lens on normalcy did not enhance my outlook on life. It only limited my ability to think differently and to be different. So, I was forced to learn how to behave and respond by fire. Meaning, I experienced blunders with friendships, relationships, and in public places that I am too embarrassed to divulge. But, I knew I had the power to reject hand me downs, which are the generational curses that are passed down from one generation to another. Alcoholism has been in my family for years. This hand me down did not start with my dad. It started in his family way before his time. This is the reason why drinking excessive amounts of alcohol is considered to be a normal recreational activity in my family. However, I refuse to maintain the status quo.

Another disease that has plagued my family is breast cancer. I could talk about this all day. However, I will not start preaching about how breast cancer attacks both men and women because this hand me down has left members of my family in deep despair. Some people grew up knowing their grandmother or shall I say Nana. Others, like me, did not have a chance. Breast cancer has attacked my family from generation to generation. It has also attacked my family on both sides. My cousin, on my dad's side, is a 1-year breast cancer survivor. My great-grandmother passed away due to complications associated with breast cancer. My grandmother passed away at the age of forty-two due to complications associated with breast cancer. My mother was diagnosed with breast cancer at the age of forty-nine and lives as a 14-year survivor who encourages others to pursue genetic testing in an effort to see if they are a gene carrier. At first, when I learned of this hand me down, I did not take it seriously. It was when I had the second mammogram that I began to take it seriously.

Being a former athlete, I had become accustomed to positive doctor reports concerning my health. I considered myself invincible. I always believed my health would be good and that any development of a disease couldn't happen to me until I was informed I had dense breast tissue, which required me to undergo additional screening. After I met with my breast cancer specialist, she asked me if I wanted to receive genetic testing. I fought and I fought genetic testing because I really did not want to know the outcome. Please keep in mind that my mom had already made several attempts to get me tested. Nonetheless, I was placed on a three month screening interval for breast cancer. I followed the screening schedule for approximately two years before I decided to move forward with the genetic testing. Yes, I was still in denial that I could possibly be a gene carrier.

During the fall of 2017, I received a call from the genetic counselor. She confirmed that I am a gene carrier for BRCA-1. I did not know what that meant. So, I asked her, "What exactly is BRCA-1?" The genetic counselor responded, "It is a breast cancer gene that could result in the development of the disease with the probability of a triple-negative strand." For those of you who are unfamiliar with breast cancer, a triple-negative strand of breast cancer means that cancer, once it develops, could be aggressive in nature. Since breast cancer runs in my family, I decided at that moment to reject this hand me down by pursuing risk reduction measures. Therefore, in the spring of 2018, I underwent my first medical procedure to have my ovaries removed. This was a huge decision because I would no longer be able to have more children.

The medical procedure sent me right into menopause. So, I began to experience what I call personal summers immediately while still in the hospital. I thought to myself, "I am a forty-three-year-old woman who has pushed herself into menopause." Although I truly did not know what all of this entailed,

I believed I made the right decision to push through the process to reduce my risk of developing breast cancer. A few months later, my breast cancer specialist scheduled me for another mammogram and ultrasound. When the results came back, she shared her concern. She stated that there was still a high chance that I could develop the disease since I still had my breast tissue and my risk factor was greater than 20% in conjunction with the BRCA-1 gene mutation.

Since there are times when men or women develop the disease between their three-month screening appointments, the doctor did not want me to take a chance. Therefore, during the Christmas holiday 2018, I experienced a prophylactic bilateral mastectomy to reduce my cancer risk further. Now, let me be clear, this does not mean I will never develop the disease. It only means that I have reduced my risk by 90 to 95 percent because it has not been proven that 100% of breast tissue can be removed ("Prophylactic Mastectomy Risks"). Therefore, as a BRCA-1 gene carrier, I must keep in mind that there is still a possibility I could develop this disease that has plagued my family for generations. However, it will not stop me from saying, "It ends here! No more hand me downs!" Let's fight the good fight against breast cancer!

If you know of generational curses that plague your family, I challenge you to put your foot down and say, "Enough!" Dare to be different and refuse to align your actions with darkness! Just because a disease runs in your family doesn't mean you have to accept that disease. Just because you were raised in a dysfunctional family, doesn't mean you can't experience functionality. Just because you were not born with a silver spoon in your mouth, doesn't mean you will never live your best life! Let's be clear! You have the POWER to change the trajectory of your life. But, you must believe in change. Just because people don't believe in you, doesn't mean you can't be who you were designed to be! There is one thing I like about history. It does **NOT** predict your future! However, *YOU* have to believe that in order to reject hand me downs!

Four Key Principles:

1) It is essential to know your history. Find out what has been passed down from one generation to the next.
2) Identify the parts of your family history that may negatively affect your behaviors and health.
3) Break the cycle of generational curses by choosing to do something different.
4) Don't settle for the status quo! **Do YOU!**

CHAPTER TWO

THE G.H.E.T.T.O. COVER STORY

"The greatest act of courage is to be in on all that you are without apology, without excuses and without any masks to cover the truth of who you truly are."

-Debbie Ford

As an adult, I often reflect on who I am as a person. I find myself battling between who I truly am and who others desire me to become. Because of my background and the environment in which I grew up, people viewed me as the "ghetto girl." This ***ghetto girl*** label has followed me all of my life. I did not choose the home I was raised in nor did I choose the neighborhood or city in which I resided. I did, however, choose to be me! This is the reason why I get annoyed when someone says, "You are *a product* of your environment." A product? What does that mean? How does a household produce or shape human behavior? How are individuals from different environments viewed? Are they viewed from a positive perspective or a negative perspective depending on that environment? You will read more about my views on the phrase, *a product of your environment*, in chapter eleven.

I used to accept what people said about me. I often agreed with the label they gave me because I did not know any better. But now, if someone calls me ghetto, I say, "You are right!" I identify myself with the G.H.E.T.T.O. because I come from a Good Healing Environment That Teaches Others! I know that I was not raised in a home with a white picket fence or born with a silver spoon in my mouth. I also know that the city that I grew up in provided a plethora of opportunities for gun violence, something that has negatively affected my family for years. However, being called ghetto without getting to know my interior, my heart, speaks to absenteeism of the mind.

Being judged by people who think they know you can be traumatizing. Just think about it. You grow up thinking that you are normal. Later on in life, you learn that only people who can identify with your background accept you. When this happened to me, I found myself making adjustments to who I was as a person. I found myself questioning my personality, questioning my urban side, which some people may refer to as the behaviors that align with the inner city, and wondering why I could not be accepted like other people. Why was it so hard for me? I refrained from being true to myself in an effort to be received by people who didn't like the real me. So, I say to you, when someone does not like who you are, they will attempt to shape you into the person they want *you* to become. When someone does not like you as a person, they will not consider your growth and development. Unfortunately, these are the same people who will put you in a box to compress your skills, talents, and personality. These are also the same people who may devalue you because they think *you* cannot soar without *them*.

But, when you know your worth, you have to dare to do you! When you know your worth, you must position yourself to become an anomaly because of the doubt you experience by naysayers. For clarity purposes, to become an anomaly, you must choose to deviate from other people's low expectations of you. So, when you know… that you know… that you know… your worth, you need to keep your head lifted high and your eyes on the prize with a sassy persona that exemplifies the necessary grit to excel in all you do! Be the anomaly! Be the *ghetto* cover story of your community! Shine like a brand new dime and let people who doubted you, realize that their lack of belief in you made you stronger and grittier in life!

I have considered myself as a leader most of my life. Who am I fooling? After experiencing bullying during my elementary years, I became a boss about my future. I decided early in life that I would not allow anyone to hold me back by degrading me and making me feel like I couldn't have the things I desired. I also decided long ago that everything I pursued in life would be pursued to the best of my ability. My push to become someone became my reality! I wanted something different. I sought to be the best version of myself. But, people can be so quick to judge you based on how you look or how you sound. People will try to judge you from your exterior without knowing who you are as a person. This judgment is difficult to embrace when your purpose in life is to operate in your gifts.

I never thought that I would have had an opportunity to lead a comprehensive high school as a building principal. This was truly a far-fetched vision of mine until I was blessed with the opportunity. When I was selected to lead the school, I thought to myself, "What a blessing to work in your passion and purpose to effect change." I also thought to myself, "Who would have ever thought this little girl from the Southside of Fort Wayne, Indiana would have a chance to lead and serve in a school with so much potential?" Leading while serving was only a dream as a child because graduating from high school and possessing a college degree was not the norm in my household. It was considered a wonder in my house. I wonder how life would be if...

To lead while you learn can be a challenge if you do not have a lens on what an effective leader looks like. You have to keep in mind that effective relationships transfer into effective leadership. If you have learned to block negative relationships in an effort to stay focused on your long-term goals, you can unintentionally block relationships that could benefit the organization or the department you lead. This was a missed opportunity I experienced as a building leader. Over the years, I grew accustomed to goal setting, goal digging, and just getting it done.

So, when it came to leading a comprehensive high school that demonstrated a need for increased student achievement, I positioned myself to move full steam ahead to accomplish the goal. This goal digging allowed me to be the G.H.E.T.T.O. girl who strived to inspire others to be all they can be without apology and regret.

Have you ever made a decision that changed the trajectory of your life? Did you work hard to get back into alignment after you took a detour in life? If your answer were yes to both of the questions above, then I would say that you understand the purpose of reflecting and rebranding to rebuild. When something is in store for you, you may not know what your preparation process will look like. Therefore, you may go through unexpected trials and tribulations that are designed to prepare you for your next best step. However, some people do not understand why your preparation period looks different from their preparation period. So when mistakes occur, you may experience a slight delay in receiving a second chance. If this happens to you, I encourage you to be patient. Although you may feel defeated while waiting on your second chance because of how hard you have worked to rebuild and rebrand yourself, you must believe that you will be given a second chance! I am here to confirm that when you are from a **G**ood **H**ealing **E**nvironment **T**hat **T**eaches **O**thers, regardless of what people think, you will have the strength to move forward as the powerhouse you were designed to be in life.

Four Key Principles:

1) You were made from your experiences and background. Now embrace your power to push forward in an effort to reach your dreams.

2) Live your best life knowing that you are better than your past.

3) Be intentional with your change process!

4) Always represent your neighborhood at the highest level by taking action to meet the needs of people that reside in the community. Be the cover story people want to read about in the neighborhood chronicles.

CHAPTER THREE

KEEP IT 100%

"I prefer to be true to myself, even at the hazard of incurring the ridicule of others, rather than to be false, and to incur my own abhorrence."

-Frederick Douglass

L eading a comprehensive high school can be a rewarding experience. Before I entered the building, I envisioned myself as being a turnaround principal that other aspiring principals would desire to emulate. However, to be that type of leader others want to emulate, you have to mix the right leadership ingredients together to be perceived as effective, relational, and inspirational. I led the way I saw others leading and that did not work for me because I was not being truthful to my own leadership skills and abilities. Turnaround leadership cannot be achieved from a top-down approach. However, it can be achieved by being your authentic self! In chapter two, I talked about how I had to mask my inner self in an effort to line up with other people's perspective of who I should become. So, when I worked as a principal that was exactly what I did. By altering my personality, I was perceived as fake. This was more than just a leadership style adjustment. It was an alteration of who I was as a person. It was an alteration of my heart. I was not being true to myself. I aligned my behaviors and belief systems with who others thought I should become. I felt like I was in a fight or flight situation and sought to operate how they thought I should operate.

When I reflected on my alteration, I saw a person who was not only fake to herself, I saw a person who was fake to her students and the staff she served. I said to myself, "This is not what transparency looks like." I was not keeping it real! So, the reflective question for you is… How can you keep it 100% if you are not 100% of who you are as a person? I believe that I failed the students and staff as a leader. I also believe that I failed them as a person! When I left, no one remembered the growth the campus experienced academically. What they remembered was a person who wasn't true to herself, which has been a long-lasting impression that has not profited my professional brand. When you lead, you need to be who you are 100% of the time to be truly effective. Other than that, you will not be effective within the organization you are leading. You will only be the person they want you to be, but you will not be true to yourself.

I have a childhood friend who taught me a lot as we grew up. As I mentioned in chapter one, I grew up in a dysfunctional household. There were a lot of times I didn't know what to do to become independent. So, this childhood friend was there for me as an adolescent and in early adulthood. She taught me how to cook certain foods and how to respond in certain situations. She witnessed me behaving abnormally at times and she was quick to tell me what was normal and abnormal. She protected me as her friend. I was deeply appreciative. But, when I got older, my childhood friend began to evaluate my actions to a fault, which ripped our friendship apart. I believe that our friendship ripped apart because I started being who I was naturally as a person and the new me was difficult to accept. The new me wasn't trying to be defiant towards her. The new me was just growing as an adult and as a genuine person. The new me was trying to be true to herself. I was trying to pave my own way, desiring to do things with passion and purpose. You are going to run across people who won't let you change for the better. But, you have to be real with yourself! *You have to keep it 100%!*

Since my personal growth, we are no longer friends. At first, it felt like I lost a loved one. I soon realized that apart from being true to myself, I needed to let go of our friendship. I needed to let go of the pain in my heart in order to accept the fact that people may be in your life for a reason and a season. So, it's okay to let go! You have to let go of people who want you to be someone else. You have to let go of people who want you to align your behaviors with the framework they have set for you. Sometimes, you have to disassociate yourself with people who are not suitable for you because they may be the ones who are holding you back. In effort to do that, you have to be true to yourself. You have to keep it real with yourself! You can't keep it real if you're not okay with being 100% of who you are as a person. People are either going to like you or love you. I guarantee, if you are 100% your authentic self, they will love you for who you are and they will give you the respect you deserve. A true friend will be there regardless! However, you have to be okay with being 100% your authentic self!

Don't mask yourself to get the job! I am not suggesting that you should be disrespectful or defiant. **Just don't lose yourself to be accepted!** You have to keep it real with yourself and everything you do should be done with passion and purpose. You have to make a strategic choice to be you! Therefore, choose to find yourself and create another opportunity for another door to open for you. Always remember... do it the right way!

Four Key Principles:

1) Keep it real to connect with the masses.
2) If you want to experience true growth, don't lose yourself to be accepted.
3) Transparency sells!
4) Do you!

CHAPTER FOUR

GOT GOALS?

"While we breathe, we will hope."

-*Barack Obama*

D are to dream! I remember being a little girl who loved to talk and loved to prove people wrong. I clearly remember sitting on my mother's porch while running my mouth like I had all the answers. I would often say, "I'm going to be a lawyer because you can't tell me anything!" Of course, things didn't work out that way. Being born in a "drop-out factory" was a challenge for me. Although education was a requirement at the primary and secondary level, once I reached a certain level, it was challenging to receive the guidance needed in an effort to prepare my mindset for post-secondary education. I was looking for a push. I needed someone to show me the way. I needed someone who had been through the grind, who could point me in the right direction. I was looking for someone who had walked the walk and talked the talk to ensure

I would reach my goal. However, I did not have anyone like that in my immediate family. So, I had to find a way to look up to other people. I found myself trying to experience inspiration through other people to take my educational journey beyond high school. What do you do when no one around you can help? You seek help to meet your needs.

Fortunately, I had an older cousin, who was a college girl. She was raised in a two-parent household all of her life. Both of her parents were active in her educational and social affairs. My cousin attended Indiana State University and became a member of Delta Sigma Theta Sorority, Incorporated. Although she loved to serve the community and demonstrated care and concern for everyone, my cousin inspired me to be more than I thought I could be. She modeled the habits of a virtuous student. She also gave me something that I did not have in my household. She gave me hope! When you grow up in a family of dropouts that usually means you will be next. However, as a product of *my* environment, I had to do something different. I did not want to be the person who had a vision and a goal with no plan to reach the goal. I wanted to be the person who beat the odds to accomplish the goal. One day, my cousin asked me about college. Of course, I didn't know how to respond because I didn't know where to start. So, she told me to begin looking at colleges to submit applications for acceptance. She also told me about a program, African American Teens on a Move (A.T.O.M.), which transported high school students to Historically Black Colleges and Universities (HBCUs).

Joining A.T.O.M. provided me with opportunities to learn about college entrance and cultural experiences that students can gain as an attendee. A.T.O.M. also inspired me to become all that I wanted to become in life. After the college visits, I believed that every goal I pursued would be reached. I felt confident that I was someone who could model, lead, and serve. They opened my eyes so that I could see the possibilities of who I could become. Let me repeat it! They opened my eyes so that I could see who I could become. To think of yourself as "becoming" someone or something was not common in my household. I developed a new outlook on my future to become someone. A.T.O.M. opened the doors for me to pursue post-secondary education at Jackson State University, majoring in Criminal Justice. This was all new to me since everyone around me experienced difficulty with completing their secondary education. But, there is one thing I learned as a first-generation college student. I learned how to connect myself with people who were leading the way to educational success!

I didn't stop pursuing my education at Jackson State University. I pursued two master's degrees and a doctoral degree. My childhood environment provided limited opportunities for people of color. Of course, there were factories in the city that paid young adults a decent salary. However, when the factory jobs were dissolved, the city experienced many laid off workers who could not afford to pay their bills. I wanted more and I knew I had to do more to get more. As it is written in the Bible, *"So, you see, faith by itself isn't enough. Unless it produces good deeds, it is dead and useless"(James 2.17)*. I knew I had to work twice as hard to get out of that environment to be accepted into a world that was new to me. I believed that if I did not pursue the un-thinkable, I would validate the beliefs of all the naysayers who doubted me. So, I stepped out to do something that had not been done in my immediate family. I pursued my high school diploma, undergraduate degree, graduate degree and doctoral degree. I developed an unstoppable desire to keep pushing! I also declared to be an anomaly so that I could demonstrate what it looks like to rebuke negative talk about your future!

But, I did not stop there either. I began to pursue jobs and positions I had only dreamed of receiving. So, if you were to ask me right now if I am a product of my environment, I am going to tell you, "YES!" I am a product of my environment because I declared that I would not align myself with the norms of the environment that have kept me in the trenches for so many years! I would not have been able to get out of my environment if I did not set goals based on a dream of becoming more than I was expected to become. I also would not have gotten out of my envi-ronment if I had not found a role model who walked the walk and talked the talk to show me the way. Let's be clear! Being a product of your environment could be the best thing for you because it's the *goal* you envision while you are in the environment. So, never stop dreaming! Never stop striving! Never stop believing!

As a college student, I often entered my roommate's room to share my goals. I would start the conversation by saying, "This is what I am going to do." When she heard the first word come out of my mouth, she already knew I was about to share a short or long-term goal I had envisioned. Although some goals never became a reality, my roommate never turned me away.

She always provided me with a strategy to work towards my goal. On the other hand, I had a friend who I would share my goals with and she labeled me dreamy. She thought I wasn't a realistic person and that my goals were just another way for me to avoid my current reality. At first, I did not think the feedback I received from my friend was negative. I truly believed the feedback was designed to save me from destruction. Years later, I realized that people can position themselves as dream killers.

People can also serve as energy vampires who take everything out of you. When I came to this realization, I decided to push forward toward my goals and not allow anyone to tell me how far I can go! I decided to develop a "do it anyway" mentality despite the naysayers and doubters. Comparable to what my mother always said, "You are not a failure unless you try!" So, when naysayers come your way to try to keep you from pursuing your goal, say, "I'm going to do it anyway!"

Four Key Principles:

1) Be consistent about goal setting.
2) Move naysayers out of the way. They are toxic to your future.
3) Demonstrate faith in reaching your end goals without hesitation.
4) Develop a "do it anyway" mentality when dealing with people who are not for you!

CHAPTER FIVE

MAKE NEIGHBORHOOD MOVES

"She didn't play the game, she changed the game!"

-Stephanie Lahart

I know you are asking yourself, "What is a neighborhood move?" When people make neighborhood moves they are leading initiatives in the community to improve the quality of life for its citizens. As a middle school student, I would always cross the pathway of an active custodian. I described the custodian as active because he was also involved in the athletic and educational affairs of students. One day, I joined the track and field program at the school. Although another staff member in the building led the track and field program, the custodian dedicated numerous hours to help shape and mold students into mentally tough student-athletes. One act of service by the custodian turned into another act of service, which, in turn, became a natural daily interaction with students.

When school ended for the academic year, the custodian invited students to join his summer Amateur Athletic Union (AAU) track and field program, Unique Track Club. Unique Track Club was not like traditional summer leagues. It was an athletic program launched to service inner-city kids in the neighborhood. The custodian, turned coach, opened and closed every practice with prayer. He also focused on character building on the weekends while traveling to track meets. I clearly remember the tough love he provided me to turn my bad attitude around. You see, the 200-yard dash was my race. As a small-framed sprinter, it was always my goal to get out of the blocks fast enough to provide me with the opportunity to focus on the curve. I spent many practices running the curves to master the lean while working on how to pump my arms strategically. During my second year as an AAU sprinter, there wasn't a track meet that I did not report to the awards stand.

Although I began to win most of my races, the attitude I displayed was not conducive to the track program. After one of the track meets, I remember the coach came up to me and said, "Cozette, you are pretty good in the 200, but there are times I wish you would lose the race." The coach's goal was not to tear me down. His goal was to get me to reflect on my negative attitude as a track athlete. The coach's goal was also to shape my character so that I could become a better athlete through personal growth. From that day forward, the coach continued his effort in refining me to become a model athlete. Believe me! It was not easy provided that I learned how to handle conflict through a dysfunctional lens. I was only one of the track members the coach shaped and molded. He helped many other track members become who they were designed to become despite their personal backgrounds. Coach Isaiah Meriweather made a neighborhood move to improve the quality of life for inner-city youth.

Youth who were part of the track program developed a passion for track and field. Therefore, any opportunity to join gangs or commit street crimes didn't serve as common obstacles for the track members. They were able to display their hidden talents on the track instead of in the street. They were also able to turn any negative energy into positive energy in an effort to push forward with their personal goals. Coach Meriweather always spoke positive to the athletes as well. It didn't matter if a runner earned first place or last place. The only thing that mattered to Coach Meriweather was that a runner finished the race. In his eyes, this built character and strength to be able to tackle the toughest issues in life. He would ask, "How did you finish?" If a runner finished strong, that is all that mattered to coach.

Coach Meriweather didn't stop at track and field. He went from mentoring youth to mentoring adults when he opened a church and began pastoring the church. Now, Pastor Meriweather serves as a family and marriage coach to help keep the family unit together. He transitioned from coaching on the field to coaching in people's homes. He kept it real and he encouraged people to reflect on their past failures as a growth opportunity to move forward. This is someone who continues to make neighborhood moves for his community.

So, I challenge you to make moves in the neighborhood you live in to make a difference in the lives of those who need you most. Making neighborhood moves is an example of how you can get gritty to overcome obstacles in the community. When you make neighborhood moves, you are helping people and it is a way to let them know that they matter! So, I leave you with this reflective question, "What move will you make to improve your community despite the naysayers?"

Four Key Principles:

1) Make moves that will add value to inner-city neighborhoods.

2) Be bold with impacting high needs communities. If something needs to be done to improve the quality of living in impoverished neighborhoods, be a part of the improvement process.

3) Be purpose-driven in everything you do!

4) Don't do it because it sounds good. Do it because it matters!

CHAPTER SIX

THE BLOCK IS HOT, STAY WOKE!

"Don't let anyone's negative opinion of you become your reality!"

-Les Brown

I don't like to reflect on my past when it brings back negative memories. However, in this case, reflecting on my past is a testament to my ability to defy negative presuppositions about me. During my freshman year in high school, I represented myself as a hip-hop fanatic. I wore baggy clothes, big shirts, salt and pepper earrings, and my hair was styled in an asymmetrical A-line. Oh yes, I compared myself to MC Lyte! When Cha-Cha-Cha would come on the radio, I was so quick to recite every lyric and was proud of it. Until one day, the Campus Resource Police Officer looked at me and said, "You are going to be trouble!" I was so devastated that I just stood there motionless near the lunch line to reflect on what he had said to me. I experienced all types of feelings! I was offended, furious, confused, embarrassed, and disappointed. I could not think of why the officer would speak about my future in such a negative manner. Then, I thought about it. Was it because of my exterior? I had never been in trouble. Therefore, I could not think of why he would choose me to target as a troublemaker.

Since I was the type of person who loved to prove people wrong, I sought to prove him wrong as well. I developed a strong intentionality on my academics. I wanted to ensure that I was focused on my studies so that I could be on the A and B honor roll. I went out for seasonal sports including volleyball, basketball, gymnastics, and track. Now, I am not saying that I was good at every sport, nor did I make every sports team I pursued. However, I was determined to be more than what the officer thought I was capable of becoming. I was determined to win at this thing called life through grit and I was not going to let someone's opinion of me become my reality!

It was not until my junior year in high school when the same Campus Resource Officer approached me and said, "You know, I was wrong about you. I remember what I said to you and I owe you an apology. You focused on *Church* and I am really proud of you!" Since *Church* was my last name, the officer called me "Church." This was a turning point for me because I knew what it felt like to be rejected by people who were not my cheerleader. I knew what it felt like to experience growth in order to endure until the end. I also knew what it felt like to become unstoppable! You can never judge a book by its cover!

There I was... a young teen who loved hip-hop culture and loved the music behind it, only to be judged by someone who did not know my heart or the vision I had for myself. I vowed never to let anyone predict my future as this would serve as a roadblock to keep me from reaching my goals. When the officer spoke negativity into my life, he ignited a flame in my soul. So, I caught fire to become the best version of myself regardless of his opinion.

I showed the Campus Resource Officer that I was an anomaly in my community. I did things he didn't think I was capable of doing. I pursued student leadership positions on campus. I was involved in clubs and organizations such as the Alpha and Omega Club and the African American Club. I also graduated as one of the top students in my class. Now, that is how you get gritty and stay gritty to reach your personal goals! I became who God designed me to become and I didn't stop demonstrating grit as a teenager. I have experienced a few tribulations, as an adult that are difficult for me to talk about in this book. However, in order for me to continue growing as a person, I have to be transparent about my past.

Almost a decade ago, I had an opportunity to work at a challenging high school. The school I was blessed to service required turnaround administrators to give birth to an aspiring culture of excellence. Before I was offered the job, I found myself questioning my skill set. I clearly remember attending a job fair, and a principal interviewed me. Of course, he was looking for an assistant principal to help lead an elementary campus. I sat with the principal eager to share my skills and talents as a data-driven leader because I believe that all students deserve a quality education. I also employed the interview strategies I learned as a Regional Principal Cohort participant. I was ready to listen, lead, and learn as a first-year assistant principal. I was ready to make a difference! However, during the interview, I got the feeling that I was not being heard as the principal barely listened to my responses, and he did not look at any of the artifacts I brought, which showcased my skills and work ethic.

I was confused. I brought the data of the Math department I led that showed exceptional growth on all grade levels. I was also confused because I had some of the best educational mentors to train me for the position I prepared to fulfill. Nevertheless, the principal looked at me at the end of the interview and said, "I would not hire you to help me lead my school. You look like you are not capable of doing anything more than market the school for me through flyers and pamphlets." My heart sank! I held back my tears because, of course, I wanted to represent myself as a strong educational leader. I then responded by saying, "Thank you for your time." I immediately got up to interview with the next principal. I did not give up!

Later that summer, I received a job offer to help lead the campus in need of turnaround leadership, adaptive practices, and culture building. This was such an awesome opportunity for me as a young administrator. Yes, the job challenged me as a leader and it provided me with an opportunity for growth professionally and personally. But, I wasn't going to let the words of the previous principal keep me from pursuing what God had in store for me. I wasn't going to let him steal my dreams of leading and learning in the schools that need us most. I also wasn't going to let doubt keep me from getting gritty for the city! I put on my full armor of God and I pushed through the leadership process as a campus leader! Two years later, I am elated to share that the English department I led on this turnaround campus, experienced academic growth in all the student groups. This was accomplished through collaborative leadership practices and trust in the teachers who believed in the vision and carried the vision into their classrooms. Not bad for someone who was only seen as a marketing clerk!

When God designed you, He designed you to be a specific person with specific talents and gifts! So, when people doubt you, I dare you to catch fire and push towards your goals anyway! I dare you to embrace all of your experiences and interactions with people to use them as stepping-stones to your next best step! I also dare you to dream even bigger knowing that someone out there doesn't think your future is for YOU! I'm aware of *self* so that I don't lose who I am to fit into a box that someone else has built for me. Don't buy into anyone else's perceptions of you unless you use it as a game-changer! Be aware of people's intent on your future! If you think differently, do different things. Stay focused by staying true to who you are and watch your fire spread!

Four Key Principles:

1) Don't buy into other people's perception of you unless you use it as a game-changer to succeed.

2) Be aware of people's intent on your future.

3) Cut off anyone who has a negative presupposition about you. Ask yourself, "What are the benefits?"

4) Seek to change people's perceptions about you by staying focused on your goals!

CHAPTER SEVEN

BREATHE! IT IS IN YOU TO SUCCEED!

"Don't be afraid of failure. This is the way to succeed!"

-LeBron James

I t is always hard to experience failure and get back up believing you can win. Sometimes, experiencing failure can lead to depression and other mental health issues. Experiencing failure can also result in a person losing their sense of self.

As an AAU track athlete with Unique Track Club, when I was testing my speed during my first track meet, I placed sixth in the 200-yard dash. You may recall, in chapter five, I talked about how I worked hard to make the 200-yard dash my best event. However, before I fell in love with the 200-yard dash, I was placed in the event on a trial basis. At the end of my very first race, my speed time resulted in a sixth-place finish. Now, I was proud of myself! I didn't know what to expect and I was just happy to receive a place on the list. I went to my dad's house to share the news. Unfortunately, my dad did not like the fact that I finished in sixth place. He did not understand that sixth place meant a lot to me because I was now good enough.

In AAU Track and Field, before you run a sprint race, you must first experience sprint trials, which consist of several heats. So, having an opportunity to run in the final sprint race is huge for many runners and placing within the top six is even better for some. I was one of the runners who was elated to have placed as one of the top six finishers. However, my dad had other feelings about sixth place. He said, "You need to place first, second, or third place to be a top finisher." Of course, since he was a former track athlete, I felt bad about finishing sixth in the race. I felt like I had failed as a track athlete. After that particular track meet, I worked hard to stay at the top of my race. I did not want to experience failure again. I knew the next weekend was fast approaching and I had to develop a mind over matter mindset. I kept telling myself, "If you at least get out of the blocks, you can have a fresh start. You may have failed in your dad's eyes, but you need to grind in an effort to experience a different outcome!" So, every practice, I would get into the blocks to envision my race. I could see myself pumping my arms and leaning the curve to win the 200-yard dash. At the end of the race, I envisioned leaning across the finish line. I did it! I was one of the top three finishers! Get behind me failure! You can't stop me now! From that day forward, I began to use track and field as a strategy to bounce back from failure.

THE GHETTO IS A LIE

In life, you will experience hills and valleys, which may affect the level of your spirit. It is easy to live your best life when you feel like you are on top of the world and when things are going well for you. However, when you experience failure, it can feel like a ton of bricks is hanging from your neck, dragging you down a dark road. Some people may feel like they are not capable of bouncing back into the swing of things because their failure experience was traumatic in nature. Failure can be embarrassing, especially if you are accustomed to positive outcomes. Failure can also take you out of the race. Therefore, when the going gets tough and you have experienced failure, I challenge you to use the following three track strategies to help you embrace failure in an effort to experience an outcome even your doubters or naysayers did not think you could experience!

Strategy #1: Get out of the Blocks

Yes! Experiencing failure is tough. When I experienced professional failure, I did not know how I was going to bounce back. It was the first time in my life I had to look at my kids to let them know that mommy didn't make the mark. It was also the first time that I felt I did not have control over my future. I could not see how I would come out of my current state of mind. Thus, I sank into a deep depression. Every day after work, I went straight home to fall asleep in a fetal position. I would literally sleep from the time I got home until the next morning for about six months. This was a very dark time in my life and I was not proud of it. I also could not control it; no matter how

35

hard I tried. I could feel the depression coming on when it was triggered and I could not figure out what the triggers were to prevent it from taking over my body. Until one day, I reflected back on the track strategies that helped me get through obstacles in my life. I said to myself, "In order to experience a fresh start, you have to get out of the blocks!" I repeated to myself, "In order to experience a fresh start, you have to get out of the blocks!

So, I began to set short-term goals that would propel me to my next best chapter. I developed a new lens to visualize who I could become in life, and I declared to be unstoppable during my rebuilding process. Although there may have been delays in reaching my short-term goals, they were not denied. I started to view every "no" as a "not right now!" I pushed and I was determined to overcome depression. I was determined to overcome failure! I was also determined to **GET GRITTY** to experience what God had in store for me! Believers take your mark… Set… Go!

Strategy #2: Pump Your Arms

After you have pushed out of the blocks for a fresh start, you may experience a smooth race until your body is fatigued. During your fresh start, you may feel like things are not going the way you thought they would go. Therefore, you may be ready to end the race! You may get frustrated because the new vision of your future is not in the plan of those who could bless you with new beginnings. You may also run across people who are unforgiving and do not believe in your rebuilding process in hopes of experiencing a second chance. Yes, these are your doubters because they don't believe in your abilities. They are your naysayers because they keep other people from blessing you. They are also your detractors because their goal is to try to keep you from staying focused on your lane to keep you from winning the race!

So, when the going gets tough, and you feel like negative people are trying to weigh you down, I need you to pump your arms and lift your legs to power through this thing called life! You got it in you! You were designed to win the race! Don't get distracted by people who don't understand your vision. Always remember, you can't tell everybody about the path you have chosen to experience greatness. There are some people who want to see you fail! But, these are the people who don't understand failure. Failure doesn't mean that it's over for you. So, when you experience failure, you will experience growth, which enriches determination. I challenge you to believe the failure hype! How do people develop grit? How do passion and purpose grow in our hearts? You are not the only person who had the monkey jump on your back in the middle of a race! Therefore, keep pumping your arms, *STAY GRITTY*, and watch how you shine at the end of the race!

Strategy #3: Lean Across the Finish Line

Approaching the end of the race may feel like an easy task. However, some people find it easy to get started on a goal and may find it hard to see it through to the finish line. I am here to tell you not to give up on your goals until you have reached the finish line. When you reach the finish line, I dare you to lean in to experience the fullness of your success! Your goals may have been just a thought in the beginning, but in the end, you will see the finish line. Hurdles may appear on the track, people may be shouting for you to win the race, and your opponents may be trying to close in on you before you reach the line. When this happens, you have to lift your knees high to clear the hurdles. Get in a zone to block out any last-minute distractions. You also have to lean in to **_FINISH GRITTY_** and experience the goal that was designed for you!

Four Key Principles:

1) Embrace failure! It is a part of the process.
2) Believe it is in you to reach your goals and be unstoppable!
3) In order to reach your end goal, you have to get out the blocks. Period!
4) If it is in you to think about it, then it is in you to go get it!

CHAPTER EIGHT

DEVELOP A DEEP DOWN PASSION TO PERSEVERE

"You can't make the scars in your life disappear, but you can change the way you see them!"

-Mark Chernoff

Growing up in a household where you learn how to handle conflict abnormally can result in unforgettable mistakes. Although human error is common, there are times when people do not allow you to experience your human side. Therefore, any mistakes you may have made in the past became a scar. The wound is reopened when people decide to dig up your past to hold it against you. In chapter one, I talked about how I witnessed domestic abuse in my family. Research states, "One-third of people who are abused in childhood become abusers themselves (Goleman)." However, I did not dive deep into my belief that children who have witnessed domestic abuse and dysfunctional relationships experience difficulty with developing and maintaining functional, healthy relationships.

Upon entering college, I experienced difficulty with developing solid, healthy relationships with the opposite sex. What did I know about positive human interaction? After all, I was accustomed to dysfunction. I was also accustomed to verbal arguments ending with domestic violence. I learned how to be rough and tough from the inside out because I had to survive in a house that was built by fear. So, when I tried to experience the dating scene in college, I must say, it did not end well. My competitive spirit mixed with my inability to talk through my concerns created a horrible concoction.

I clearly remember getting off work on a Saturday evening. The cab driver dropped me off on the yard. As soon as I got out of the cab, I saw a male student I had grown quite fond of over time. Although I was fond of the male student, I did not want him to know how much I liked him. So, I created distance between us until I was ready. Unfortunately, the distance was too far as evidenced by his decision to move on to another relationship. When I realized our opportunity had expired, I experienced difficulty with accepting the new status of our relationship. My inability to embrace this reality led to embarrassment and a severed budding close friendship. It was too late to start over. It was too late to recover the friendship I once cherished. I was at a loss! I thought to myself, "Why didn't you handle it differently?" I had no answers, as I was not taught how to nurture a healthy relationship as a child.

Twenty-five years later, I ran into an old classmate who knew about the situation. Of course, he did not go down memory lane with me. He decided to reminisce with his friends after I left the room. He used the story as a mockery while questioning how I was able to move forward in life, knowing the mistake I made years ago. Fortunately, the friends he shared the story with knew me as a person. They knew I must have grown from the incident, as they had never witnessed such behavior since they've known me. You see, my friends have known me for more than twenty years as well. Therefore, they were able to speak to my character and heart. They have seen me persevere through obstacles. My friends were also able to speak to what they have witnessed in my marriage from the outside, which is support, laughter, and love. Fortunately, my mistake was no longer the core of the joke. It served as an example of how people can change and learn from the inside out in their most vulnerable moments.

People will try to keep you from shining and moving forward by bringing up your past. They want to send the message, "She is not all of that!" But, we must all remember that no one is perfect and we have all made mistakes we are not proud of in life. If someone brings up an embarrassing moment you experienced in your past to make a mockery out of you, that person is not your friend nor does that person have anything inspiring going on in his or her life. Although you can't change your past, you can use your past to develop into the person God designed you to be in life. You can also use your past as a way to build wisdom and possibly keep someone else from making the same mistake. Always remember, "*all things*" are designed to work together for your good, no matter how they feel (Rom. 8:28)! So, I challenge you to embrace your mistakes and look at them as learning experiences instead of demotions of character.

Four Key Principles:

1) Don't let anyone push your past into the present.
2) Your scars are your learning experiences. So, grow and go get it!
3) If someone tries to use your past to describe you, then that person doesn't know what it takes to be made.
4) All things work together for the good (Rom. 8.28)! All things!

CHAPTER NINE

MAINTAIN AN ALPHA AND OMEGA MINDSET

"These claims are valid even though I make
them about myself. For I know where I came
from and where I am going, but you do not know
this about me."

(John 8.14)

Have you ever met someone who devalued you before they got a chance to really get to know you? Did they see your worth? If not, please know that the person you met sized you up to determine how far they thought you would go as a professional or in life. People like that are accustomed to judging a book by its cover or may I say... judging people by their exterior. They focus on the exterior with no desire to look inside. In this book, I've shared how I grew up in a dropout factory. I have also shared the hip-hop side of me and how I masked myself in an effort to be accepted professionally and socially. Please don't get this confused with the code-switching concept. For those of you who are not familiar with the term, I consider code-switching as an individual's ability to change their behavior or language style based on the environment he or she encounters to be viewed as appropriate for that environment without losing their sense of self. See, I lost my sense of self. Therefore, I considered the strategy I employed to be more so in alignment with masking.

I truly believe that some people experience difficulty with accepting how people are molded. These are people who try to put you in a box because they do not believe that you can make it without their assistance. If you do make it, these are the people who want to uncover how you did it because they don't believe you made it as a result of your natural skills or talents. These are people who feel they can control your destiny. They don't value you or believe you have the ability to step up to the challenge to move organizations or tasks forward. Just because you run into people who don't value you, doesn't mean you don't have value. Just because people don't believe in your ability doesn't mean you can't do it. When you come across someone who gives you a difficult time because of what they think they know about you, I dare you to be noticed without being noticeable! Don't worry about what they think because they don't define you nor do they understand the experiences that made you!

Be okay with people not believing in you! If you continue to seek man to accept you, especially when they do not believe in you and you know you have a gift, you must continue to push past the process and stay focused. One day, what you desire to be and what you desire to do, will happen! It may not happen through the person who does not believe in you. It may not happen through your friends that you are hanging out with because they may not believe in you! It may not happen with the organization you are working for because that organization may not be for you. But, it will happen! So, you have to ensure that whatever skill-set you demonstrate, you continue to be the best version of YOU!

From the words of my personal mentor, Dr. Sheri Miller-Williams, "Trust the process!" People have a tendency to judge you by your exterior. They may not believe in you and lowered your value rating when you can actually be the key person in the organization to help it grow! You may be the hidden gem needed to launch a major initiative within the organization. You can be the hidden gem to mobilize the community in supporting change so that the organization can thrive and grow in the desired direction! Even if you are the hidden gem, people will judge you! Therefore, you must have an Alpha and Omega mindset because your beginning may have been rough, but it does not predict your end! You have to believe that what is for you is for YOU! Bottom line! When God is ready to bless you, there is not a devil in hell that can keep the blessing from you! If you don't believe me, just watch the blessings flow when you let go and truly believe in what God can do!

You have to believe that you are more than capable of performing the service and leading the charge within an organization! You are more than enough! I will say it again, "YOU ARE MORE THAN ENOUGH!" If you are in a relationship and someone treats you like you are not good enough, do you stay in the relationship? Some people decide to stay in toxic demeaning relationships. But, is it beneficial to stay in a situation that is not good for you? Who is getting the most from you? You have to know that you are good enough! When someone treats you like you are not good enough, you have to say to yourself, "You may know about my beginning and you may have witnessed the valley I experienced, but that does not dictate my end!" This is what an Alpha and Omega, a beginning and an end, mindset looks like! You must develop an Alpha and Omega mindset to push through negativity! You must keep an Alpha and Omega mindset to withstand the evil that may confront you when you are pumping your arms to persevere through tough situations! *YOU ARE MORE THAN ENOUGH!*

One day, I contacted a family member to see how she was doing. I had not heard from her in quite some time since I now live in the South. She knew that I had recently completed my doctoral program. So, she asked, "What are you going to do next?" I responded by saying, "I am not sure. I may return to Real Estate since it is my second passion." My family member then responded by saying, "Well, I don't think that education is your thing. I think you are a better Real Estate agent. Real Estate is what you are good at and it is where you can experience success!" Okay, now I had to clutch my pearls! I did not know how to respond as I developed a deeper passion, over the years, to serve as an educator.

In addition, as a goal digger, I have always tried to refrain from telling anyone what *I* thought they weren't good at, especially if it could potentially be hurtful. Now, I truly believe that my family member did not mean any harm by voicing her opinion. However, hearing her evaluate my performance as an educator and a real estate professional was upsetting because her evaluation was not supported by data. Thus, I reflected on the following statement, "You can't change the people around you, but you can change the people you choose to be around" (Bennett)!

From that point on, I decided that I was not going to let anyone speak negativity into my aspirations. I also decided not to ever let anyone hold me back. After all, you can be all you desire to be in life! When I am focused on a goal, I run in my own lane so that I can finish the race strong without apology and without excuse!

Four Key Principles:

1) Don't let anyone tell you how far you can go. Do it anyway!

2) Know your worth and believe it is of great value!

3) Be a beast about dreaming big! Who is it going to harm?

4) Stay on track with your dreams. Don't run the risk of disqualification when someone tries to run in your lane!

CHAPTER TEN

GET COMFORTABLE WITH BEING UNCOMFORTABLE

"Whenever you feel uncomfortable, instead of retreating back into your old comfort zone, pat yourself on the back and say, "I must be growing," and continue moving forward."

— T. Harv Eker

Growing can be uncomfortable! Sometimes you can experience a certain level of discomfort when you are trying to take your life to the next level. Sometimes you may want to turn back around because things are unfamiliar to you. You may say to yourself, "I'm not feeling this!" As humans, we seek to experience spiritual growth as if it is something tangible. We also want that feeling to be comfortable. However, being stretched and experiencing growth to take your life to the next level may feel uncomfortable. As I mentioned before, when I pursued the college of my choice, I was uncomfortable. I met friends who came from well-educated families and education was a top priority in their household. The way they talked about pursuing post-secondary education to obtain a degree was an unfamiliar conversation for me. You see, I grew up in a small city where most African-American adults worked in refineries. They earned a decent salary and were able to take care of large families with the money they earned. Therefore, education was a far-fetched idea that only the privileged discussed.

At the age of 18, young black adults were already earning at least $50,000 a year. At such a young age, earning $50,000 was considered a very high salary. In my opinion, earning $50,000 a year is still a decent salary for many families! So, it is just that I chose to take a different path. I was not accustomed to being around friends who were raised in two-parent households. I was not accustomed to having table talk about white-collar careers and African American trailblazers who paved their way to success! I was also not accustomed to talking to young African American girls who never held a food stamp in their hand. This was all new to me! As you can see, I had a small lens when it came to understanding the true struggle of African Americans and how we have overcome adversity to have more and be more with each generation. I also realized that we were behind in the Midwest region. Why did we allow the refineries to define what success looked like or felt like in the city? Although the money earned by the employees at the refineries created opportunities for them to take care of their families and travel, this demonstration of success was temporary in nature because it was only experienced as long as the refineries were up and running.

It was such a culture shock to gain a new understanding of what we, as a race, were capable of doing in the community. Of course, people may read books to learn about history. However, I was never around so many black and brown students with a vision of what success looks like! As a result, my personal experience gave me a limited perspective. I was very uncomfortable! I was not accustomed to dressing up to attend class as this was the norm at Jackson State University and it caught me by surprise. I was comfortable wearing baggy clothes and Used Jeans. If you were born after 1985, you may not be familiar with the Used Jeans brand. I was also comfortable wearing two-tone jumpers with one strap hanging in the back and colored hair. I was comfortable with just being me!

As I grew up at Jackson State University, I grew out of the hip-hop version of myself into a young professional adult. I found my place in the community to make connections with kids and people of similar backgrounds. Yes, I was uncomfortable at first! However, my experience with being uncomfortable refined me into an educator who is unapologetically passionate about closing the achievement gap. The term achievement gap refers to "any significant and persistent disparity in academic performance or educational attainment between different groups of students such as white students and black students or higher-income and lower-income students" ("Achievement Gap"). My experience with being uncomfortable encouraged me to develop an unstoppable mentality to reach my goals. My experience with being uncomfortable also shaped me into a fearless go-getter who refuses to let anyone prevent me from living my best life and living it abundantly!

If you are working on a job and you feel like your boss is always on your case and you have not been given the recognition you deserve, you must continue to perform with passion and always remember that you have to stand strong because this level of discomfort is preparing you for your next best opportunity! You have to persevere through this process. If you are comfortable, then you are not growing! You may feel like you are in the furnace. But, when you come out, you will be well done!

I challenge you to think about when you prepare a meal for baking. The label on the package may suggest you bake the meal for at least 45 minutes. This is the time it will take to cook the meal. When you walk away from the oven, I can assure you that when the oven reaches a specific temperature the food will begin to cook. The temperature in the oven will create an environment in which the meal can go through a process towards refinement. This process is comparable to the process you may experience when you are undergoing refinement. You may open the oven from time to time to poke the meal to see if it is well done. If it needs a little more time, you will need to close the oven so that it can continue the process. Once again, this is comparable to the process we go through as humans.

When it's time for you to grow, you may experience things that will not be comfortable. You may not like the process you are going through to experience refinement. However, you must keep in mind that your feeling of comfort may lead you to a spirit of complacency even when your current situation is not good for you. So, don't be afraid to experience pain to reach your end goal. Get comfortable with being uncomfortable if you want to experience true growth!

Four Key Principles:

1) Expect to be uncomfortable when you are being stretched.

2) Seek unfamiliarity to experience growth.

3) A comfortable feeling can lead to complacency even when your current situation is harmful.

4) Being uncomfortable can be painful. However, experiencing pain can help you reach your end goal!

CHAPTER ELEVEN

DON'T BE SCARED TO BE THE ANOMALY

"Think outside of the box. Work outside of the box.
Dream outside of the box. Succeed outside of the
box."

-Matshona Dhliwayo

In chapter two, I expressed my concerns about comments I often hear about people who are raised in at-risk communities. I questioned the meaning behind "product of your environment." When someone says that another person is a product of his or her environment, it leaves a negative feeling in my spirit. It also leads me to question their thinking process and how they actually view the person they are referencing. So, what does it mean? Let's dig a little deeper in this chapter. Being a product of your environment means that your environment may have shaped you and it may have molded you into the person you are today. But, it does not mean that your behaviors align with the environment. You can be a product of your environment and take the least traveled path because of what you learned in the environment. You can be a product of the environment because you know about it and you desire to evoke change in the environment. So, being a product of your environment is not supposed to carry a negative connotation.

People should not say that you are a product of your environment if their mindset leads them to believe that you are just like your environment. I am a product of my environment. I was born in a dropout factory. I experienced alcoholism in my family. I know what it looks like, smells like, and I know how it behaves. Being a product of my environment did not make me like my environment. It empowered me to desire to do things differently. It also empowered me to take the least traveled path so that I could help those who have been where I have been and help those who are trying to do something different. Being a product of my environment empowered me to be brave. It helped me push past the doubters! It helped me push past the naysayers! It helped me push past the people who tried to run in my lane!

It was because of my environment that I wanted to be different in an effort to give kids in the community someone to look up to or aspire to be like. I wanted to impact the community in such a way to make connections with people and send a clear message that they matter! Who would have thought that this little girl who grew up in a dropout factory would earn a doctoral degree? *Dare to be different!* I also dare you to challenge people when you hear them say that someone is a product of their environment. People can put a label on you without con-crete evidence to support their rationale for the label. If this happens, stay focused on who you are designed to be in life. It's okay if your environment shaped or molded you to be different! But, don't allow anyone to talk down to you about what they think in regards to how you compare to your environment.

It doesn't matter if someone in your family has experienced teenage pregnancy or incarceration. Often, the person making the statement does not know you. Nobody knows your story better than you know your story. Therefore, no one knows how your story will end! You may have experienced trauma in your life, which resulted in low grades at school, low energy at work, or low appetite. That gives no one a reason to develop a negative presupposition to define you! Seek strategies to become who you were designed to become! Use what someone says against you for your good! *DARE TO BE DIFFERENT!*

Four Key Principles:

1) Being a product of your environment is perceptual in nature.
2) Your behaviors may be shaped by your childhood en-vironment. However, your actions align with the path that you chose!
3) Take the least traveled path to break the cycle.
4) Do something no one expects you to do even if you are the only one doing it!

CHAPTER TWELVE

THAT'S GAME!

*"It's the player that makes the hand, not the hand
that makes the player."*

-Dr. Tonya Curtis

Everyone is dealt a deck of cards in life. Sometimes I look at life like it is a game. I say that because there are times when you may feel like you have been dealt a bad hand in life. You may feel like you can't catch a break and you are always faced with trials and tribulations. I have learned that in life, you can't look at the blessings of others and think your blessing is not on the way. You also cannot compare your experience with someone else's experience. There may be something else in store for you that required you to experience multiple tribulations so that you can come out well-built and prepared to lead the charge. I mentioned earlier how I experienced a professional setback. Although I now consider my setback as a learning experience, I decided to look at it like a deck of cards to decide what card I would play next. So, I played a few cards to help me win the game. Of course, no one thought that I would be in the game this long. However, I am still at the table as a strong player in the game and I refuse to let another player trump me!

It's hurtful to experience one closed door behind another closed door. Some of you know what I am talking about! You get your hopes up thinking that your chapter of disappointment is almost over only to learn that the chapter you are living has a few more pages in it. Thus, you are still going through the journey. Although you are accomplishing goal after goal, you are still not given a second chance. But, because you understand the game, you keep playing because you have faith that one day you will be able to throw in a spade and say, "That's game!"

Someone I hold dear to my heart experienced a deep valley in her life. It seemed like everything was about to crumble before her eyes. She began to experience difficulty in her personal life and work-life at the same time. It would have been easy for her to walk away. But, she decided to play one of the cards she was dealt. She didn't worry about the jokers out there! She didn't worry about being trumped! She just stayed focused on what she needed to do, based on her passion and purpose in life. She played the card nobody expected her to play! She deviated from the norm because she knew what she needed to do, and she wasn't going to let anybody tell her how far she could go! She thought about it. Set her personal goals and pushed forward to accomplish the goals despite the naysayers and doubters. She did it anyway!

Until this day, she is still at the table. She still has a good hand. She is not looking at the bad card she was dealt and she is still winning! It was not the card she was initially dealt. It is how she played her hand! It is how she persevered! It is how she dodged the joker! She did not let anyone become the comedian in her life! So, it's not about the cards that you're dealt. It's about playing your hand strategically! An unknown author stated, "I didn't grow up having role models. I grew up having people I didn't want to be like and seeing situations I'd never want to be in. Not all of us are dealt the right cards, but that doesn't mean you can't reshuffle your deck for a better outcome"("The Minds Journal").

Sometimes, negative situations can consume you. You may experience one thing after another. You could say, "Oh my gosh!" "I lost my job!" "Oh my goodness!" "My boyfriend broke up with me!" A close friend can deviate from your life and it can feel like things are falling apart. Comparable to a deck of cards, you got to look at your experiences to see how you are going to play this game called life so that you can still be a strong player at the table and win. So that you can still get up victoriously and still say that you are who God says you are and you're going to be who God says you will become! Believe that you are the strongest player at the table! I dare you to tell yourself, "I will be better today than I was yesterday!" You are going to be a person who's going to persevere! You *will* become unstoppable, but you got to stay in the game! You cannot give up! Play your card to win!

Four Key Principles:

1) Don't be afraid to pull out your trump card to win this game called life.

2) Always consider your hand as the winning hand.

3) Stay ready for the joker. He is nothing but a comedian. He has no value in your life!

4) If it's a spade, call it a spade and keep it moving!

CONCLUSION

To experience true growth, you have got to be brave enough to admit your mistakes and bold enough to reflect on your past failures. You must also identify the ingredients that made you. Everyone's behavior and personality is developed by their childhood experiences and sometimes the childhood experiences may be a result of generational curses or misfortune. So, it is imperative that you dig deep to discover the recipe that developed you into the person you are today.

Think about how you will reject generational curses in effort to live the life that was specifically designed by your creator? Also, think about how you have responded to failure in the past. Did you look at it as a learning experience or did you accept it as a part of life? It is my belief that failure is designed to break you down in an effort to set you up for the breakthrough of your life! It's not the fact that you have experienced failure; it's how you respond to it to become a better version of yourself.

Never let anyone tell you how far you can go! You must believe in yourself and dare to take a different path in life. If it weren't for my childhood experiences, the doubt voiced by nay-sayers, or the long talks with my AAU coach, I wouldn't be able to say, "In order to achieve, *YOU* must believe!" Now, go get it!

REFERENCES

"Achievement Gap." *The Glossary of Education Reform: For Journalists, Parents, and Community Members.* Great Schools Partnership, 2014, Web. 28 Dec. 2019.

Bennett, Roy T. "The Light in the Heart." *Goodreads.com*, n.d. Web. 28 Dec. 2019.

Brown, Les. *BrainyQuote.com*, n.d. 28 Dec. 2019.

Chernoff, Marc. "8 Thing to Remember When Everything Goes Wrong." *Before It's News*, https://beforeitsnews.com/opinion-liberal/2019/09/8-things-to-remember-when-everything-goes-wrong-6-2-2596196.html. Accessed 28 December 2019.

Dhliwayo, Matshona. *Goodreads.com*, n.d. Web. 28 Dec. 2019.

Douglass, Frederick. *Goodreads.com*, n.d. Web. 28 Dec. 2019.

Eker, T. Harv. *AZQuotes.com*, n.d. Web. 28 Dec. 2019.

Ford, Debbie. "Courage: Overcoming Fear and Igniting Self-Confidence." *Goodreads.com, n.d. Web. 28 Dec. 2019.*

Goleman, Daniel. "Sad Legacy of Abuse: The Search for Remedies." *New York Times*, Jan 24, 1989. Web. 28 Dec. 2019.

James, LeBron. *AZQuotes.com*, n.d. Web. 28 Dec. 2019.

Lahart, Stephanie. *Goodreads.com*, n.d. Web. 28 Dec. 2019.

New Believer's Bible Compact: First Steps for New Christians. New Living Translation. Carol Stream: Tyndale House, 2009. Print.

Obama, Barack. *Goodreads.com*, n.d. Web. 28 Dec. 2019.

"Prophylactic Mastectomy Risks." *Breast Cancer.org, Sept 14, 2017, Web. 28 Dec. 2019.*

"The Minds Journal." n.p, n.d. Web 28 Dec. 2019. https://the-mindsjournal.com/i-didnt-grow-up-having-role-models/

www.ingramcontent.com/pod-product-compliance
Lightning Source LLC
Chambersburg PA
CBHW031044110426
42740CB00048B/1181